GEORGIA'S AMAZING COAST

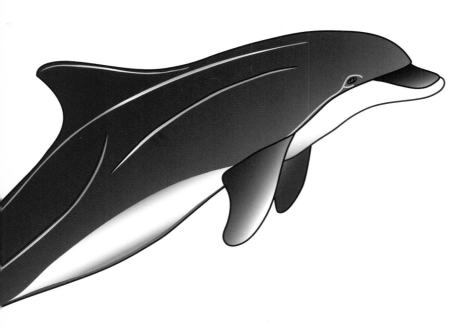

GEORGIA'S

NATURAL WONDERS FROM ALLIGATORS TO ZOEAS

AMAZING COAST

BY DAVID BRYANT AND GEORGE DAVIDSON

ILLUSTRATED BY CHARLOTTE INGRAM

PUBLISHED IN COOPERATION WITH GEORGIA SEA GRANT

THE UNIVERSITY OF GEORGIA PRESS | ATHENS AND LONDON

© 2003 by the University of Georgia Press
Athens, Georgia 30602
All rights reserved
Designed by Charlotte Ingram

The paper in this book meets the guidelines
for permanence and durability of the Committee
on Production Guidelines for Book Longevity
of the Council on Library Resources.

Printed in China
07 06 05 04 03 P 5 4 3 2 1

Library of Congress Cataloging-in-Publication Data available

British Library Cataloging-in-Publication Data available

ACKNOWLEDGMENTS

Charlotte Ingram created the beautiful illustrations in this book and is also responsible for the book's design. George Davidson, a talented musician, artist, and writer, and I wrote the text. This book originated as a project of Georgia Sea Grant, which supports coastal research, education, and outreach in Georgia. Part of the National Sea Grant College Program, Georgia Sea Grant is funded by the National Oceanographic and Atmospheric Administration and the University of Georgia and is part of the School of Marine Programs at the University of Georgia. Georgia Sea Grant Director Dr. Mac Rawson was instrumental in providing the resources and support that made this project possible. We also received a great deal of research assistance from the University of Georgia Marine Extension Service.

INTRODUCTION

Perhaps the most amazing thing about Georgia's coast is that it moves. It's moving now, but as amazing as that movement is, you can't watch it happen. It's a spectacle that unfolds in geological, rather than Eastern Standard, time. However, in a watchful moment, you can discover evidence of this ancient wandering in the intricate and beautiful web of life it leaves behind. Regulated by the freezing and thawing of polar ice caps, Georgia's shoreline moves inland for a few million years, and then back out again, rolling back and forth across itself. It has traveled upward as far north as the fall line, a range of low hills that runs between Augusta, Macon, and Savannah, and as far out to sea as the edge of the continental shelf. This constant motion makes Georgia's coast unique, for unlike the coasts of, say, Maine or Oregon, it has no hard edge. Once inside the shifting sand of the barrier islands, Georgia emerges from the sea as a soggy band of estuaries and tidal marsh that extends inland for miles. Only deep inland do you find anything you might plant your feet on or your crops in and for any practical purpose call "land." And it is this wide intermingling of land and sea, salt water and freshwater, fisherman and farmer that creates a fabulously rich nursery for marine and terrestrial creatures. This book celebrates that richness.

Today, Georgia's coast is less than a hundred miles long, but it contains one-fourth of the salt marsh on the United States' eastern coast.

This marsh provides a stable and safe haven for the breeding and hatching of an enormous number of sea creatures. Its murky shallows protect these animals during their embryonic and juvenile stages from the hazards of the open sea. Rivers nurture the young with nutrients drawn from as far away as the North Georgia mountains. This abundance of marine life, in turn, promotes a thriving and diverse population of terrestrial creatures at the margin of land and sea. We humans are part of that thriving population, and we compete with other species for space and resources. We've been very successful, but we must understand that our increasing dominance affects the very resources for which we compete.

The facts and features collected in this book provide only a sampling of the boundless natural wonders along Georgia's coast. An understanding and appreciation of the coastal environment is especially important for Georgians, most of whom live at least a hundred miles from the shore. Our hope is that familiarity with the marvels of Georgia's coast will promote a sense of stewardship in all those whose activities, upstream or along the water's edge, affect the health of this fragile intertwining of life and geology. Most of all, we hope that this book will delight its readers and inspire in them a curiosity to learn more about Georgia's amazing coast.

David Bryant
Director of Communications
Georgia Sea Grant

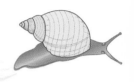

GEORGIA'S AMAZING COAST

ALLIGATOR

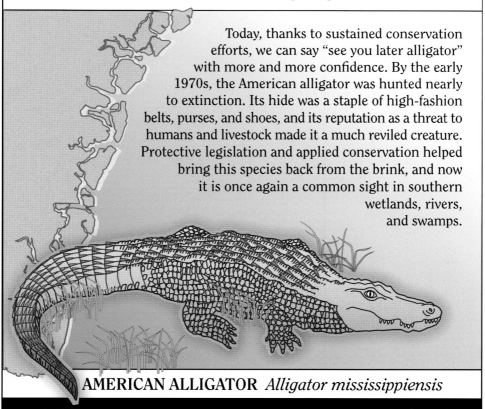

Today, thanks to sustained conservation
efforts, we can say "see you later alligator"
with more and more confidence. By the early
1970s, the American alligator was hunted nearly
to extinction. Its hide was a staple of high-fashion
belts, purses, and shoes, and its reputation as a threat to
humans and livestock made it a much reviled creature.
Protective legislation and applied conservation helped
bring this species back from the brink, and now
it is once again a common sight in southern
wetlands, rivers,
and swamps.

AMERICAN ALLIGATOR *Alligator mississippiensis*

ALLIGATOR HOLE

Many people "dig" the American alligator and have helped increase its numbers through conservation efforts, but not many realize that the alligator also helps by digging, too. It digs holes, "gator holes" to be exact. These large depressions in the bottoms of ponds and marshes serve a vital function during dry times of the year and particularly during periods of drought. Fish, frogs, birds, and mammals rely on these "wells" for survival since the holes are dug into the groundwater level and remain even after adjacent waters have dried up. They provide a reliable source of fresh water for drinking and a habitat for fish.

ALLIGATOR HOLE

ARMADILLO

With its interconnected armor plates covering both body and tail, the nine-banded armadillo appears to be bulletproof. A survey of roadkill along coastal Georgia highways proves otherwise, however, as this sedentary and nearly blind burrowing mammal trails only the oppossum as the most frequent roadside wildlife fatality. Originally introduced to Florida in the early 1900s, the armadillo expanded its range to include the coastal plains of Georgia by the 1960s. Its diet consists largely of insects and other invertebrates, some plants, and occasionally bird eggs. As part of our diets, armadillo meat is pleasingly palatable but quite rich.

NINE-BANDED ARMADILLO *Dasypus novemcinctus*

AVOCET

This long-legged migratory shorebird makes its home in Georgia for part of the year. Also known as "blue shanks" because of its bluish-gray legs and feet, the avocet has a distinctive upturned beak, which it uses with great flourish. When feeding, it thrusts its bill underwater and sweeps it vigorously from side to side, stirring up a frenzy of insects and crustaceans for dinner. Dramatic defenders of their nests, avocets are avian thespians. Their acting "routines," designed to distract predators from their eggs and young, range from a soulful "Call Me Mr. Pitiful" to the kamikaze dive bomber, which usually sends inquiring eyes and noses elsewhere fast!

AMERICAN AVOCET *Recurvirostra americana*

BLOOD ARK

Although it has not gained widespread acceptance in America, the blood ark clam is considered quite a delicacy on the worldwide sushi market. Today, however, the Georgia variety of this unusual bivalve is sold only in ethnic markets in the U.S. Its name derives from the fact that, like humans, its blood contains hemoglobin, which gives it a reddish color. The periostracum, or covering on the outer part of the shell, serves two purposes. It extends outward slightly from the edge of the shell and helps keep the blood ark from sinking down into the mud, and its slippery surface discourages predation since interested diners find it difficult to grasp. As American palates broaden, expect to see the blood ark making its mark on seafood cuisine!

BLOOD ARK *Anadara ovalis*

BLOOD WORM

The blood worm, sometimes called the clam worm, is a marine relative of the common earthworm. But it maintains its own peculiar sort of detachment during the reproductive process. During spring, blood worms enter a reproductive phase and form a tail segment at the end of the body, which is filled with either eggs or sperm. Shortly after the full moon, these tail segments, or epitokes, detach and rise to the surface. The resulting spawning event presents quite a spectacular sight. Billions of wormlike shapes gyrate wildly near the water's surface. The vigorous motion releases the eggs and sperm into the water, where the eggs are fertilized. The eggs develop into larvae, which drift with the tides and feed – or are fed upon – until they grow to juvenile worms and return to the bottom, where they spend the majority of their lives.

BLOOD WORM *Neanthes succinea*

BLUE CRAB

With bright blue coloring along its frontal area, it's obvious where this common Georgia crab gets its name. Like other members of the Decapod order, it has five pairs of legs. The first pair is a set of powerful claws, and the last is flattened into a paddle-like shape for swimming. As a hunter, particularly of oysters and hard clams, it is ferocious, and as the hunted, it makes ferociously good eatin'. Whether prepared as freshly made crab cakes or left whole in their soft-shell stage, blue crab is a highlight of coastal cuisine.

BLUE CRAB *Callinectes sapidus*

BOTTLENOSE DOLPHIN

Though still fairly plentiful on Georgia's coast, the bottlenose dolphin is susceptible to the pollution and habitat alteration that are on the rise. Hopefully, its inclusion under the umbrella of the Marine Mammal Protection Act will insure that this delightful creature is a common coastal denizen for generations to come. With a length of 6 to 12 feet and weighing as much as 1,450 pounds, it's no surprise that bottlenose dolphins must consume 15 to 30 pounds of fish, squid, and crustaceans a day to fuel their acrobatic routines. This intelligent creature has its own language – echolocation. It emits a series of of high-pitched clicks and senses the sound waves as they bounce off objects, such as dinner.

BOTTLENOSE DOLPHIN *Tursiops truncatus*

CABBAGEHEAD JELLYFISH

The most common jellyfish in Georgia waters is the cabbagehead. It can reach 8 inches in diameter, and because it looks spherical when washed up on the beach, it is also known as the cannonball. Like other jellyfish, it uses a venomous sting to paralyze its prey. Fortunately for swimmers, it is one of the least dangerous of its kind. Instead of the long tentacles of other species, it has short, sticky folds, called arms, with which it captures the larvae of clams, oysters, and crustaceans. Humans who come in contact with these arms get an annoying but generally harmless sting. Jellyfish drift aimlessly with the current, so if you have a painful collision with one, you share the blame.

CABBAGEHEAD JELLYFISH *Stomolophus meleagris*

CHACHALACA

Called the "Mexican pheasant," the chachalaca was introduced on the Georgia coast by hunters as a game bird. It is native to Central America, and its natural range is from Costa Rica to Texas. The species did not thrive here, so chachalaca hunting never quite caught on, but a small number of birds has managed to breed and maintain a population on Sapelo and Little Saint Simons Islands. The chachalaca reaches 20 to 24 inches in length and has dark brown wings, a buff underbelly, and a darker tail. This highly social bird's raucous call of "cha-cha-laca" can be heard as it perches in the forest canopy at dawn and dusk. These days it is more likely to be seen through a bird-watcher's binoculars than through a hunter's sights.

PLAIN CHACHALACA *Ortalis vetula*

CLAPPER RAIL

Coastal visitors are more likely to hear this bird "rail" than to see it. A wary inhabitant of Georgia's tidemarsh, the clapper rail, or marsh-hen, is actually quite abundant despite its rare appearance. From its nest in thick grasses above the high-water mark, it ventures along innumerable paths amidst marsh vegetation, usually at top speed, as it searches for food – small crabs, snails, insects, and some plants. Weak of wing, this large bird ($14\frac{1}{2}$ inches high) swims well and can dive underwater for sustained periods. In the spring, adult rails are hunted by humans during extra-high tides, appropriately called "marsh-hen tides."

CLAPPER RAIL *Rallus longirostris*

COQUINA BIVALVE

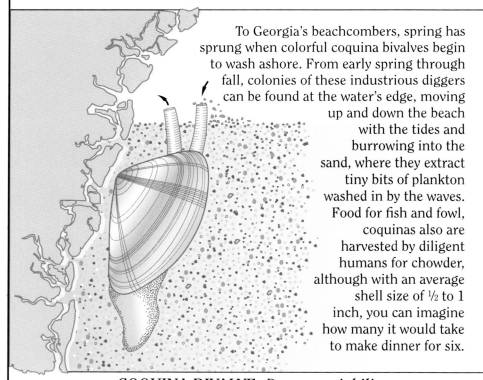

To Georgia's beachcombers, spring has sprung when colorful coquina bivalves begin to wash ashore. From early spring through fall, colonies of these industrious diggers can be found at the water's edge, moving up and down the beach with the tides and burrowing into the sand, where they extract tiny bits of plankton washed in by the waves. Food for fish and fowl, coquinas also are harvested by diligent humans for chowder, although with an average shell size of ½ to 1 inch, you can imagine how many it would take to make dinner for six.

COQUINA BIVALVE *Donax variabilis*

COW KILLER

Also called the velvet ant because of the tiny hairs covering its body, the cow killer is in fact a wingless wasp that can be found in Georgia's coastal zone. This striking species is a shocking shade of red and has two black bands at its abdomen. Cow killers are solitary, which means they have no central hive or nest. The female deposits her eggs in the hive of another species, and her larvae feed off those of the resident bees – quite a presumption on the hospitality of strangers! Only the female is capable of stinging, but with a name like "cow killer," well, let's just say humans should definitely stay out of her way!

COW KILLER *Dasymutilla occidentalis*

COYOTE

While they may be home on the range, the range is not their only home. In fact, coyotes have become quite numerous in Georgia's coastal plain. Introduced into this area by fox hunters, coyotes enjoy their place on the food chain – that of top dog. Their only predators are humans and packs of wild dogs. Frequently, their large dens – sometimes 10 to 30 feet in length – are expanded and "remodeled" tunnels they've taken over from armadillos and gopher tortoises. The female produces one litter, averaging five pups, per year. Once the pups are weaned, mom and dad bring food back in a very personal container – their stomachs – and disgorge it for their pups to enjoy.

COYOTE *Canis latrans*

DEER FLY

Buzz-ZZZ-zz-ZZZZ-zzz-ZZ. Round and round your head buzz several flies despite your attempts to flee or shoo them away with flailing arms and hands. After a couple of blood-raising stings you regret your decision to explore the marsh's edge. You are the victim of the deer fly. Not much larger than a house fly, the deer fly is mostly black or yellow with bright green or yellow eyes. While the male peacefully gathers nectar and fruit juice, the female saws into your skin and sucks your blood. She has sawlike mandibles for this job and an anticoagulant saliva that keeps blood flowing even after she's had her fill. On hot, still summer days these little vampires await the unsuspecting mammal in foliage near streams and wetlands. Beware.

DEER FLY *Chrysops* spp.

DIAMONDBACK RATTLESNAKE

The eastern diamondback is the largest and deadliest of the world's thirty-two species of rattlesnakes. Found in coastal Georgia's palmetto flatwoods and pine-lands, the snake has a natural diamond-shape pattern of browns to black that provides full-time camouflage. Like other pit vipers, the eastern diamondback gives birth to live young. When born, the young average 14 inches. With fully functional fangs and venom, they're ready to kill and eat an adult mouse. Long considered a scourge, the eastern diamondback is not aggressive to humans unless cornered. But humans are a threat to the eastern diamondback – while numerous snakes have fallen victim to motorists and rattlesnake roundups, far more have been killed by habitat degradation and development practices. Today, its population numbers and range have shrunk dramatically. It's possible this rattler has not gotten a fair shake!

EASTERN DIAMONDBACK RATTLESNAKE *Crotalus adamanteus*

DIAMONDBACK TERRAPIN

Unlike sea turtles or its inland terrapin cousins, the diamondback terrapin thrives in a brackish mixture of fresh and salt water that is plentiful in Georgia's marshes and estuaries. There, it nests on small marshy islands and eats mostly snails. It gets its name from the intricate pattern on its shell. Once prized for its succulent flesh, it was almost hunted to extinction. With turtle soup now out of fashion, the diamondback has grown plentiful in Georgia and can often be seen crossing coastal roadways, where it falls prey to its current chief predator, the automobile.

DIAMONDBACK TERRAPIN *Malaclemys terrapin*

EASTERN INDIGO SNAKE

Federally listed as a threatened species since 1978, the eastern indigo snake is one of the largest nonpoisonous snakes in North America. It feeds on a variety of prey – birds, young turtles, frogs, and other snakes, including the rattlesnake. Prior to federal protection, the commercial pet trade took a heavy toll on wild populations because of the indigo's good-natured reputation. Today, habitat loss and degradation have reduced populations of the eastern indigo beyond the minimum required to sustain the species. This companionable reptile often overwinters, along with other snakes and small mammals, in a gopher tortoise burrow; it sometimes even has another guest for dinner – of course the unfortunate guest is the "special du jour!"

EASTERN INDIGO SNAKE *Drymarchon corais*

FIDDLER CRAB

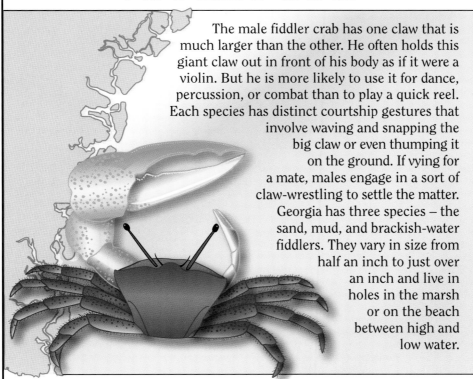

The male fiddler crab has one claw that is much larger than the other. He often holds this giant claw out in front of his body as if it were a violin. But he is more likely to use it for dance, percussion, or combat than to play a quick reel. Each species has distinct courtship gestures that involve waving and snapping the big claw or even thumping it on the ground. If vying for a mate, males engage in a sort of claw-wrestling to settle the matter. Georgia has three species – the sand, mud, and brackish-water fiddlers. They vary in size from half an inch to just over an inch and live in holes in the marsh or on the beach between high and low water.

MUD FIDDLER CRAB *Uca pugnax*

FLYING SQUIRREL

Contrary to the aerial stunts of its cartoon manifestation (that is, Rocky the Flying Squirrel, of *Rocky & Bullwinkle* fame), this tiny mammal doesn't fly at all – it glides. A membrane known as an alar, which runs along its body from wrist to ankle, creates a winglike surface when the squirrel spreads its limbs. It uses these "wings" to glide from tree to tree – usually no more than 30 to 50 feet, although glides of 100 to 200 feet have been reported. Common in the pine forests of Georgia's coastal plain, this nocturnal creature has huge eyes and sensitive night vision. Rarely on the ground for long, it forages primarily in treetops and along trunks and branches for its diet of nuts, berries, fungi, bird eggs, and insects.

SOUTHERN FLYING SQUIRREL *Glaucomys volans*

FOSSILIZED SHARK TOOTH

Georgia's official state fossil, the fossilized shark tooth, presents compelling evidence that much of Georgia was once under the sea. The state's oldest shark teeth are more than 65 million years old. Then, sharks shared the world with dinosaurs. In that distant past, the sea covered the southern half of the state, so the oldest fossils are generally found far from today's coast, on land now covered with trees, cattle, crops, or cities. We find only the sharks' teeth because sharks lack true bone and have a skeleton made of cartilage. Only the teeth have the hard calcium necessary for fossilization.

FOSSILIZED SHARK TOOTH

FRANKLINIA ALTAMAHA

In 1765, King George III's Royal Botanist to North America, John Bartram, and his son William discovered a grove of camellias like none they'd ever seen growing on the banks of coastal Georgia's Altamaha River. They named it for their friend and fellow Philadelphian Benjamin Franklin. Several years later William visited Georgia again and returned home with seeds of the delicate shrub to plant in the botanical garden of his Philadelphia home. In doing so, Bartram unwittingly saved it from extinction. The *Franklinia altamaha*'s beautiful white and yellow blossom hasn't been seen in the wild since 1803. All known remaining plants were propagated from those in Bartram's garden. A recent census found only about two thousand of these descendants in homes and gardens around the world.

CAMELLIA *Franklinia altamaha*

FREE-TAILED BAT

Despite its small, narrow wings, the free-tailed bat is the fastest flier among American bats. Just try following its dizzy flight path as it catches up to 3 grams of insects a night – not a bad sky patrol above the boggy wetlands of Georgia's coastal plain! Unlike most other bats, this species has a tail that extends well beyond its body, which gives it the odd appearance of an aerial mouse. Georgia's free-tailed bat colonies, usually numbering several thousand or fewer bats, are far smaller than those in the southwestern U.S. Like their western kin, they have a pungent, musky odor emanating from glands in the skin.

BRAZILIAN FREE-TAILED BAT *Tadarida brasiliensis*

FRESHWATER SLOUGH

Pronounced like "slew," this feature of coastal Georgia's salt-marsh ecosystem is actually an oasis of sorts. Sometimes these sloughs are only small, temporary ponds that disappear during dry periods, but often they are larger permanent ones. Formed when the surface of the ground and the water table coincide, freshwater sloughs provide habitat and nesting and feeding grounds, as well as a source of fresh water, for the numerous species of birds, amphibians, reptiles, and mammals that depend on these coastal oases for survival. You'll find them in dune meadows, marsh hammocks, maritime forests, and the shrub zones of beaches.

FRESHWATER SLOUGH

FRIZZLE CHICKEN

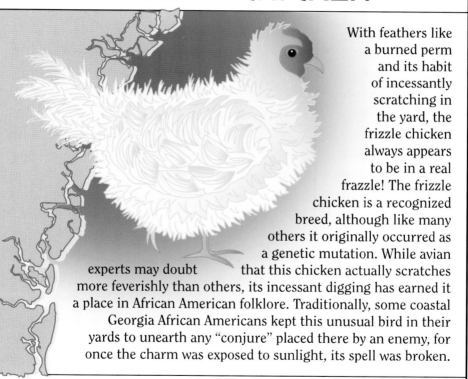

With feathers like a burned perm and its habit of incessantly scratching in the yard, the frizzle chicken always appears to be in a real frazzle! The frizzle chicken is a recognized breed, although like many others it originally occurred as a genetic mutation. While avian experts may doubt that this chicken actually scratches more feverishly than others, its incessant digging has earned it a place in African American folklore. Traditionally, some coastal Georgia African Americans kept this unusual bird in their yards to unearth any "conjure" placed there by an enemy, for once the charm was exposed to sunlight, its spell was broken.

FRIZZLE CHICKEN *Gallus gallus*

GAFFTOPSAIL CATFISH

This unusual catfish cuts a striking figure in Georgia estuaries with its long filament-like streamers that extend from its pectoral and dorsal fin spines and from its jaw. Looks aside, however, the gafftopsail's most distinctive characteristic is its method of reproduction. Its eggs are close to an inch in diameter, which isn't very impressive unless you take into account the fact that males of this species incubate a mouthful of them for up to two months or until the young can fend for themselves. By that time the young are nearly 3 inches in length, which speaks volumes about dad's tight-lipped but tender nurturing!

GAFFTOPSAIL CATFISH *Bagre marinus*

GEORGIA'S TIDES

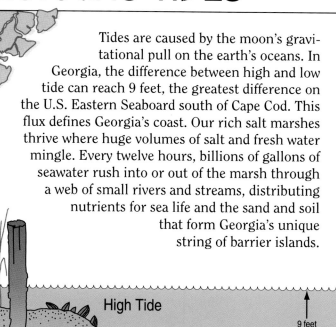

Tides are caused by the moon's gravitational pull on the earth's oceans. In Georgia, the difference between high and low tide can reach 9 feet, the greatest difference on the U.S. Eastern Seaboard south of Cape Cod. This flux defines Georgia's coast. Our rich salt marshes thrive where huge volumes of salt and fresh water mingle. Every twelve hours, billions of gallons of seawater rush into or out of the marsh through a web of small rivers and streams, distributing nutrients for sea life and the sand and soil that form Georgia's unique string of barrier islands.

High Tide

9 feet

Low Tide

GEORGIA'S TIDES

GHOST CRAB

The ghost crab, common to Georgia's sandy beaches, is one of the few crabs that stands erect on the tips of its legs. These pale, grayish-white creatures are not usually seen during the day but emerge at night from their burrows just above the high-tide mark to scavenge for rotting plant or animal detritus. Ghost crabs are also formidable predators with sharp, powerful claws that can crush small shellfish. Their tiny black eyes on the ends of long vertical stalks give them a very alert, if not startling appearance. Don't blink when you see one; this fleet-footed crab just might disappear into thin air, rather like a ghost.

GHOST CRAB *Ocypode quadrata*

GHOST SHRIMP

The ghost shrimp's translucent white color and its notably "shy" nature give this coastal Georgia denizen a mysterious air. Its pale coloration is due to an absence of pigment, which is typical of subterranean animals. This diligent creature digs its own burrow, an elaborate, often intertwining network of tunnels, and rarely ventures outside. And, like for many of us, its "housework" is never finished, since it is constantly cleaning and expanding its burrow. The ghost shrimp doesn't have to travel far to enjoy a meal. It extracts bacteria and detritus from mud for nourishment.

example of burrow with fecal matter at entrance

GHOST SHRIMP *Callianassa major*

GLASSWORT

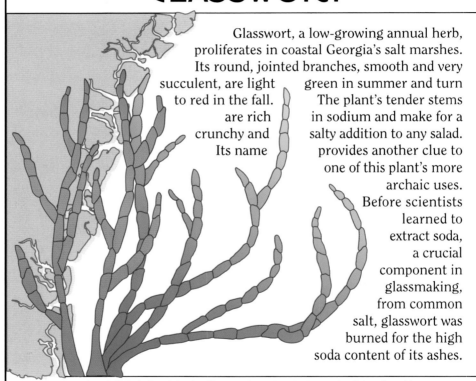

Glasswort, a low-growing annual herb, proliferates in coastal Georgia's salt marshes. Its round, jointed branches, smooth and very succulent, are light green in summer and turn to red in the fall. The plant's tender stems are rich in sodium and make for a crunchy and salty addition to any salad. Its name provides another clue to one of this plant's more archaic uses. Before scientists learned to extract soda, a crucial component in glassmaking, from common salt, glasswort was burned for the high soda content of its ashes.

GLASSWORT *Salicornia virginica, S. bigelovii*

GOLDEN SILK SPIDER

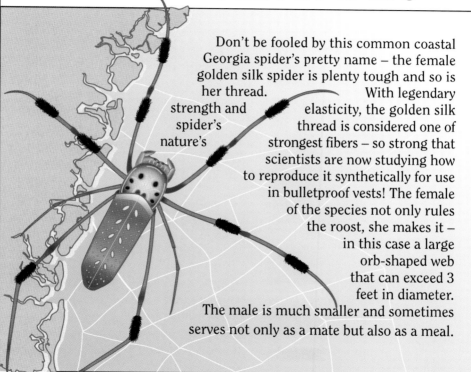

Don't be fooled by this common coastal Georgia spider's pretty name – the female golden silk spider is plenty tough and so is her thread. With legendary strength and elasticity, the golden silk spider's thread is considered one of nature's strongest fibers – so strong that scientists are now studying how to reproduce it synthetically for use in bulletproof vests! The female of the species not only rules the roost, she makes it – in this case a large orb-shaped web that can exceed 3 feet in diameter. The male is much smaller and sometimes serves not only as a mate but also as a meal.

GOLDEN SILK SPIDER *Nephila clavipes*

GOPHER TORTOISE

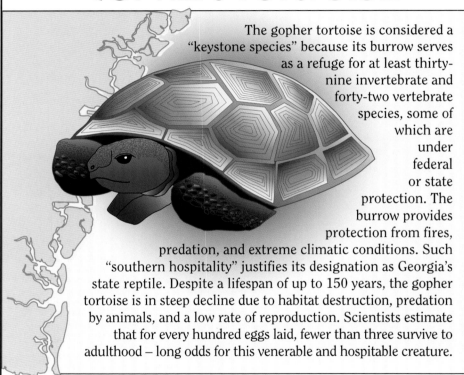

The gopher tortoise is considered a "keystone species" because its burrow serves as a refuge for at least thirty-nine invertebrate and forty-two vertebrate species, some of which are under federal or state protection. The burrow provides protection from fires, predation, and extreme climatic conditions. Such "southern hospitality" justifies its designation as Georgia's state reptile. Despite a lifespan of up to 150 years, the gopher tortoise is in steep decline due to habitat destruction, predation by animals, and a low rate of reproduction. Scientists estimate that for every hundred eggs laid, fewer than three survive to adulthood – long odds for this venerable and hospitable creature.

GOPHER TORTOISE *Gopherus polyphemus*

GRAY'S REEF

Gray's Reef lies about 17 miles east of Sapelo Island. It is a vast complex of underwater limestone outcroppings that rise up to 10 feet above the ocean floor. This habitat of caves, burrows, troughs, and overhangs attracts a wide variety of bottom-dwelling and free-swimming marine life. The reef is particularly valuable to loggerhead sea turtles, who use it to forage and to rest, and it is also part of the designated calving grounds for the endangered right whale. The reef has archaeological interest as well. Gray's Reef was once a barrier island just off Georgia's coast. Fossil evidence indicates that it was populated by paleo-Indians and large mammals such as sabertooth tigers and mastodons. Gray's Reef is now a national marine sanctuary.

Gray's Reef

GRAY'S REEF *A National Marine Sanctuary*

GREAT BLUE HERON

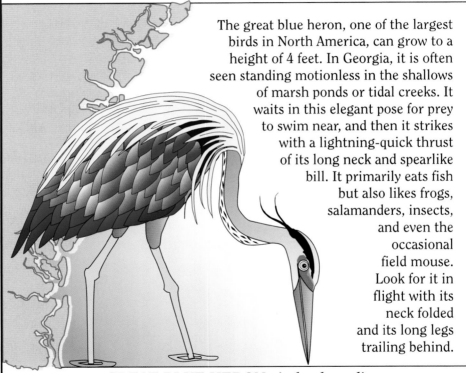

The great blue heron, one of the largest birds in North America, can grow to a height of 4 feet. In Georgia, it is often seen standing motionless in the shallows of marsh ponds or tidal creeks. It waits in this elegant pose for prey to swim near, and then it strikes with a lightning-quick thrust of its long neck and spearlike bill. It primarily eats fish but also likes frogs, salamanders, insects, and even the occasional field mouse. Look for it in flight with its neck folded and its long legs trailing behind.

GREAT BLUE HERON *Ardea herodias*

GREEN TREE FROG

With its smooth, bright green-to-olive skin, the green tree frog is a striking ornament in its habitat of foliage at the water's edge. Although small, 1 ¾ to 2 ½ inches, this creature can leap distances of up to 10 feet using legs that are 1 ½ times the length of its head and body. Unlike frogs that spend most of their lives in the water, the green tree frog's toes are not webbed. Instead, the end of each toe has an adhesive pad, which is used in climbing. Come early May, Georgia's coastal marshes and swamps echo with the nocturnal chorus of male frogs serenading the females. This amorous clamor is no sweet song, however, since it is said to resemble the sound of a cowbell!

GREEN TREE FROG *Hyla cinerea*

HOGNOSE SNAKE

The eastern hognose derives its name from the unique upturned scale at the end of its snout. This feature suggests a hog's nose and is just the thing for burrowing in the loose, sandy soil that is the snake's preferred habitat. In Georgia, accurate population studies of this furtive species have proved difficult since it is fossorial, which means it spends much of its life underground. When threatened, the hognose musters all the bluster it can and, hissing loudly, spreads the ribs just behind its head such that it resembles a cobra. If this display doesn't discourage predators, this thespian will play dead instead.

EASTERN HOGNOSE SNAKE *Heterodon platyrhinos*

HOODED PITCHER PLANT

Helping to even the score a bit for the plant kingdom, the hooded pitcher plant eats animals. With the promise of nectar, this plant lures ants, bees, butterflies, and other insects deep inside its tubular leaves, where they are introduced to an inverted kink in the food chain. Crawling insects are guided to a pool of fluid at the bottom of the tube by sharp, spiny, downward-pointing hairs that keep them there until they drown and decompose into nutrients for the plant. Flying insects fare no better. Once inside, they think light shining through translucent spots on the plant's tube signals an exit, and after much confused fluttering – splash – another heartless vegetarian meal is avenged.

HOODED PITCHER PLANT *Sarracenia minor*

HORSE CONCH

Of considerably greater size than its next largest kin, the horse conch can grow to 2 feet in length. In Georgia, this marine snail occurs primarily in offshore waters but occasionally is washed ashore by severe storms. In the world of marine snails, the horse conch is king not only because of its immense size but also because it is a fierce predator. Its shell, a grayish-white to salmon color, has a thin, brown, flakey covering called a periostracum, and the inside of the shell's aperture is a brilliant orange or red.

HORSE CONCH *Pleuroploca gigantea*

HORSESHOE CRAB

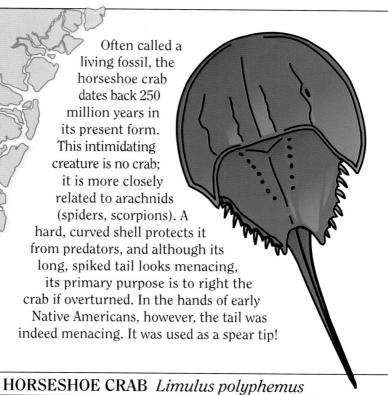

Often called a living fossil, the horseshoe crab dates back 250 million years in its present form. This intimidating creature is no crab; it is more closely related to arachnids (spiders, scorpions). A hard, curved shell protects it from predators, and although its long, spiked tail looks menacing, its primary purpose is to right the crab if overturned. In the hands of early Native Americans, however, the tail was indeed menacing. It was used as a spear tip!

HORSESHOE CRAB *Limulus polyphemus*

ISLAND GLASS LIZARD

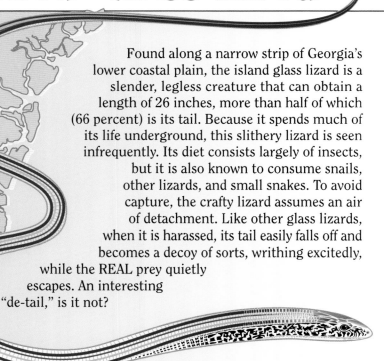

Found along a narrow strip of Georgia's lower coastal plain, the island glass lizard is a slender, legless creature that can obtain a length of 26 inches, more than half of which (66 percent) is its tail. Because it spends much of its life underground, this slithery lizard is seen infrequently. Its diet consists largely of insects, but it is also known to consume snails, other lizards, and small snakes. To avoid capture, the crafty lizard assumes an air of detachment. Like other glass lizards, when it is harassed, its tail easily falls off and becomes a decoy of sorts, writhing excitedly, while the REAL prey quietly escapes. An interesting "de-tail," is it not?

ISLAND GLASS LIZARD *Ophisaurus compressus*

KINGFISHER

With its pointed beak thrust forward, the belted kingfisher patrols its river or stream at high speed and low altitude. Though sleek and graceful in the air, it appears awkwardly top-heavy when perched on a limb. It looks as if the head, beak, and neck of a large and powerful predator were stuck by mistake on the body and small feet of a common blue jay. But there's a reason for this anatomical imbalance, for unlike the osprey or eagle, the kingfisher hunts with its beak, not its feet. This solitary hunter catches a fish in its beak, returns to its perch, knocks the fish against a convenient limb to stun it, then flips the fish in the air and swallows it whole. Apparently, this is what becomes of table manners when you eat alone.

BELTED KINGFISHER *Ceryle alcyon*

KNOBBED WHELK

"Housed" in Georgia's state seashell, the knobbed whelk is a marine gastropod commonly found in intertidal mudflats and offshore in waters up to 30 feet deep. Its shell whorls, or coils, clockwise and grows to a length of 9 inches, making this whelk one of the largest sea snails on the coast. A hard-working predator, the whelk uses the lip of its shell to pry open its bivalve prey, then inserts its proboscis and begins feeding. This method of dining damages the shell, so adult whelks are constantly reconstructing their dwellings. It's easy to see why this creature takes a beating while eating!

KNOBBED WHELK *Busycon carica*

LAUGHING GULL

Something of a trickster, the laughing gull is known to steal fish from the beaks of pelicans. Perhaps that is one reason for its pronounced call, a piercing "ha ha ha." Colonies of this crow-sized gull are found in Georgia's isolated coastal tidal marshes. During the summer months, the adult laughing gull's head and broken white eye-ring suggest a bandit in flight as it searches for food over marshes, mudflats, and beaches. During the winter, its head turns gray. For humans, this would be no laughing matter, but for the laughing gull, it's just another joke. "Ha ha ha."

characteristic black

LAUGHING GULL *Larus atricilla*

LEATHERBACK SEA TURTLE

The world's largest sea turtle, the leatherback, can reach 6 to 8 feet in length and weigh as much as 2,000 pounds! Unlike those of other sea turtles, the leatherback's shell is not rigid but is made up of many small, bony plates covered by a leathery skin. It also has the unusual ability, for a reptile, to maintain a core body temperature that is higher than its surroundings. That explains how it can range from the tropics to Georgia's coast to the icy waters of Greenland. Its diet seems a recipe for painful indigestion: it eats only jellyfish.

LEATHERBACK SEA TURTLE *Dermochelys coriacea*

LIVE OAK TREE

The live oak is Georgia's state tree. It gets its name by keeping its leaves throughout the winter, long after other oaks have lost theirs. It drops most of its leaves in spring and begins replacing them almost immediately. Georgia's earliest settlers, including founder General James Oglethorpe, wrote of the live oak's great beauty and dense canopy. It is truly a magnificent tree. With widespread and twisting limbs, its horizontal reach often exceeds its height. Typically shrouded in Spanish moss, it gives the coastal landscape a dreamy and romantic look.

LIVE OAK TREE *Quercus virginiana*

LONGFIN INSHORE SQUID

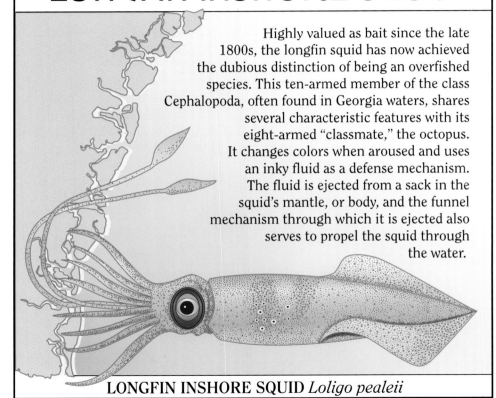

Highly valued as bait since the late 1800s, the longfin squid has now achieved the dubious distinction of being an overfished species. This ten-armed member of the class Cephalopoda, often found in Georgia waters, shares several characteristic features with its eight-armed "classmate," the octopus. It changes colors when aroused and uses an inky fluid as a defense mechanism. The fluid is ejected from a sack in the squid's mantle, or body, and the funnel mechanism through which it is ejected also serves to propel the squid through the water.

LONGFIN INSHORE SQUID *Loligo pealeii*

LONGLEAF PINE FOREST

Longleaf pine forest once dominated the coastal plain of Georgia by cooperating with wiregrass and lightning. Its tall, straight trees attract lightning, which ignites the wiregrass on the forest floor. The resulting low fire merely scorches the trunks of most longleaf pines, whose high limbs are above the flames' reach, but destroys the seedlings of competing tree species, leaving the forest free of undergrowth, a condition favorable to the pines' companion plant, wiregrass. Longleaf seedlings survive by developing roots for years before they leap for the sky, growing up to 6 feet a year, pushing their crowns out of danger between fires. Logging, agriculture, and population change have now almost done what fire and lightning couldn't – eliminate the longleaf ecosystem in Georgia.

LONGLEAF PINE *Pinus palustris*

MANATEE

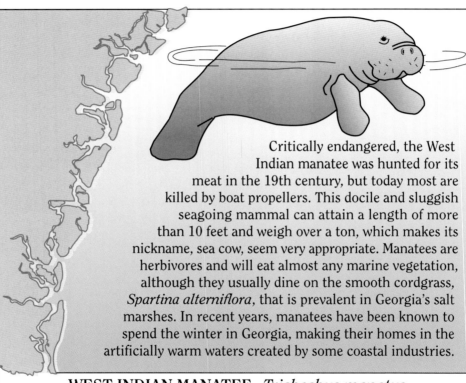

Critically endangered, the West Indian manatee was hunted for its meat in the 19th century, but today most are killed by boat propellers. This docile and sluggish seagoing mammal can attain a length of more than 10 feet and weigh over a ton, which makes its nickname, sea cow, seem very appropriate. Manatees are herbivores and will eat almost any marine vegetation, although they usually dine on the smooth cordgrass, *Spartina alterniflora*, that is prevalent in Georgia's salt marshes. In recent years, manatees have been known to spend the winter in Georgia, making their homes in the artificially warm waters created by some coastal industries.

WEST INDIAN MANATEE *Trichechus manatus*

MARINE BACTERIA

Bacteria get a bum rap. Sure, there's *E. coli* and a few other troublemakers, but for every bacterium that's up to something bad, there are millions up to something good. In fact, you could say bacteria run the environment. They perform the most elemental tasks in the cycles of nature, breaking down organic matter and other compounds into components useful to the smallest creatures of the food web and releasing gases that regulate climate. Scientists believe that a newly discovered family of bacteria, the *Roseobacter* lineage, may account for as much as 30 percent of the bacteria in Georgia's estuaries. These bacteria turn the sulfur in seawater into the amino acids that build proteins, as well as into a gas that counters the greenhouse effect. So, you might want to think twice about being anti-bacterial.

MARINE BACTERIA *Sagittula stellata (Roseobacter* lineage*)*

MARSH HAMMOCK

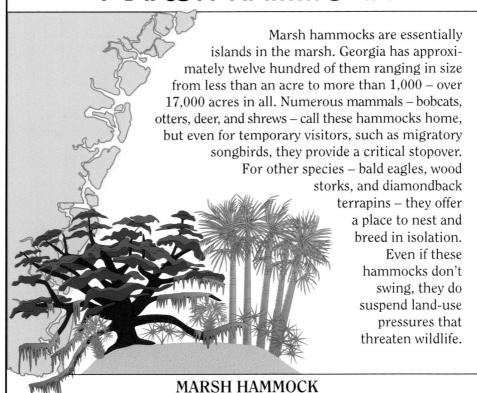

Marsh hammocks are essentially islands in the marsh. Georgia has approximately twelve hundred of them ranging in size from less than an acre to more than 1,000 – over 17,000 acres in all. Numerous mammals – bobcats, otters, deer, and shrews – call these hammocks home, but even for temporary visitors, such as migratory songbirds, they provide a critical stopover. For other species – bald eagles, wood storks, and diamondback terrapins – they offer a place to nest and breed in isolation. Even if these hammocks don't swing, they do suspend land-use pressures that threaten wildlife.

MARSH HAMMOCK

MARSH MUD

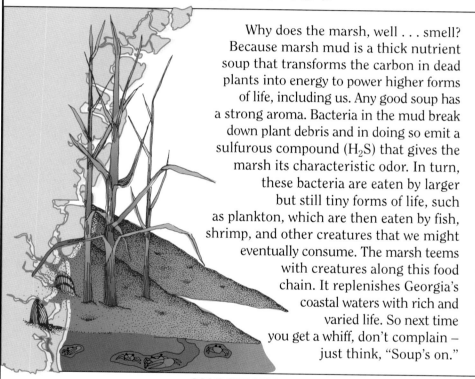

Why does the marsh, well . . . smell? Because marsh mud is a thick nutrient soup that transforms the carbon in dead plants into energy to power higher forms of life, including us. Any good soup has a strong aroma. Bacteria in the mud break down plant debris and in doing so emit a sulfurous compound (H_2S) that gives the marsh its characteristic odor. In turn, these bacteria are eaten by larger but still tiny forms of life, such as plankton, which are then eaten by fish, shrimp, and other creatures that we might eventually consume. The marsh teems with creatures along this food chain. It replenishes Georgia's coastal waters with rich and varied life. So next time you get a whiff, don't complain – just think, "Soup's on."

MARSH MUD

MARSH PERIWINKLE

Common to Georgia's salt marshes, the marsh periwinkle is no flower but instead is a member of a group of marine gastropod mollusks that are characterized by their conical, spiraling shells. At low tide these snails can be found at the base of one of their favorite foods, the smooth cordgrass, *Spartina alterniflora*, which is the predominant plant in Georgia marshes. However, as the tide rises, so does the periwinkle. Up the cordgrass stalk it goes, where in turn, it sometimes becomes food for sharp-eyed egrets and herons.

MARSH PERIWINKLE *Littoraria irrorata*

MARSH RABBIT

Smaller and darker than its more common cottontail cousin, the marsh rabbit's fur is a deep reddish brown on its back and gray to buff-colored on its underbelly. Its small tail is gray-brown, and its ears are somewhat shorter than those of the cottontail. This furtive creature's habitat includes coastal and freshwater marshes, lowland meadows, swamp borders, and river and creek banks. Marsh rabbits are powerful swimmers and have been seen swimming as far as ¼ mile from shore, but perhaps their most distinctive feature is the ability to stand up and walk on their hind legs! Numerous predators consider this rabbit a tasty meal, and heavy rains can flood its lowland habitat, drowning young rabbits and nestlings. Parenting these bunnies must be a HARE-raising experience!

MARSH RABBIT *Sylvilagus palustris*

MARSH RICE RAT

Rice is one of this nocturnal rodent's favorite menu items. That's evident from its genus name, *Oryzomas*, which means "rice" in Greek. Though rice is nice, this creature is no snob. A true omnivore, it also chows down on seeds, snails, crustaceans, insects, bird eggs, and the tender parts of aquatic plants and marsh grasses. Usually found in brackish salt marshes along Georgia's coast, this medium-sized rodent is semi-aquatic. It can swim on top of the water or dive beneath it to avoid capture or to sup on succulent plant life. In addition to hawks, owls, and snakes, humans are also a predator of the marsh rat, albeit inadverenty. As undisturbed coastal areas give way to development, this rat's habitat shrinks along with its numbers.

MARSH RICE RAT *Oryzomys palustris*

MARSH WREN

In spring, the Georgia marsh echos with the cheerful "ch-ch-ch-ch" of marsh wrens. Though they are both numerous and vocal, you may not see one. The marsh wren, a scant 4 inches from beak to tail, spends its life inside the grass canopy of the marsh, rarely touching the marsh floor and making only brisk, buzzing flights above the grass on little wings. There in its green world it forages for insects and snails and makes hanging, globular nests in the marsh grass. Using a "hide the thimble" routine to confuse predators, the wren may build several nests, but it deposits eggs only in one.

MARSH WREN *Cistothorus palustris*

MOON SNAIL

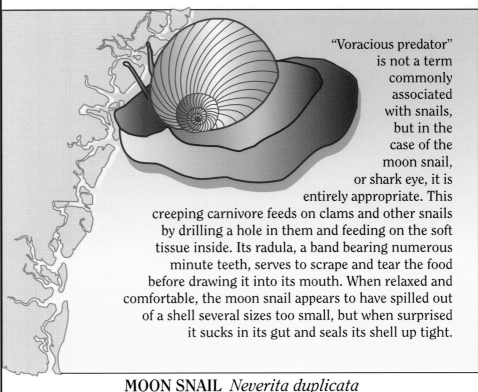

"Voracious predator" is not a term commonly associated with snails, but in the case of the moon snail, or shark eye, it is entirely appropriate. This creeping carnivore feeds on clams and other snails by drilling a hole in them and feeding on the soft tissue inside. Its radula, a band bearing numerous minute teeth, serves to scrape and tear the food before drawing it into its mouth. When relaxed and comfortable, the moon snail appears to have spilled out of a shell several sizes too small, but when surprised it sucks in its gut and seals its shell up tight.

MOON SNAIL *Neverita duplicata*

MORNING GLORY

Throughout Georgia, the sun is greeted and dismissed each day by the opening and closing of morning glories. The state's hundreds of species include the sweet potato plant. There are two prominent coastal varieties – the pink railroad vine and the white fiddle-leaf morning glory. Both are also referred to as beach morning glories and flourish on sand dunes and the upper beach, often right up to the water's edge. The railroad vine also likes the hard scrabble along railroad tracks. There is little more elegant in nature than the gentle, twisting open and close of the morning glory in response to the sun.

Railroad Vine Morning Glory
Ipomoea pes-caprae

Fiddle-leaf Morning Glory
Ipomoea stolonifera

MORNING GLORY *Ipomoea* spp.

MOSQUITOFISH

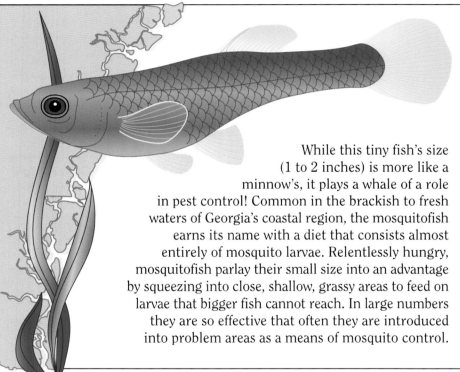

While this tiny fish's size (1 to 2 inches) is more like a minnow's, it plays a whale of a role in pest control! Common in the brackish to fresh waters of Georgia's coastal region, the mosquitofish earns its name with a diet that consists almost entirely of mosquito larvae. Relentlessly hungry, mosquitofish parlay their small size into an advantage by squeezing into close, shallow, grassy areas to feed on larvae that bigger fish cannot reach. In large numbers they are so effective that often they are introduced into problem areas as a means of mosquito control.

MOSQUITOFISH *Gambusia affinis*

OCTOPUS

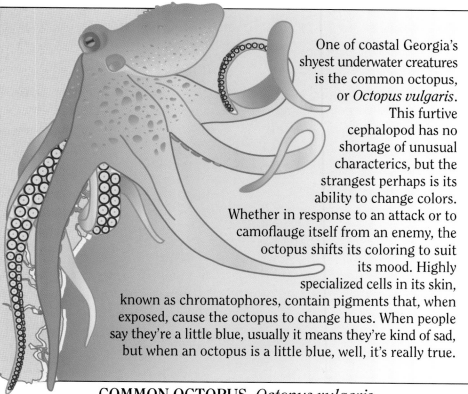

One of coastal Georgia's shyest underwater creatures is the common octopus, or *Octopus vulgaris*. This furtive cephalopod has no shortage of unusual characterics, but the strangest perhaps is its ability to change colors. Whether in response to an attack or to camoflauge itself from an enemy, the octopus shifts its coloring to suit its mood. Highly specialized cells in its skin, known as chromatophores, contain pigments that, when exposed, cause the octopus to change hues. When people say they're a little blue, usually it means they're kind of sad, but when an octopus is a little blue, well, it's really true.

COMMON OCTOPUS *Octopus vulgaris*

OPOSSUM

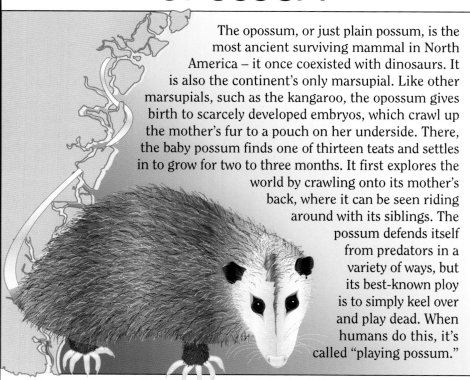

The opossum, or just plain possum, is the most ancient surviving mammal in North America – it once coexisted with dinosaurs. It is also the continent's only marsupial. Like other marsupials, such as the kangaroo, the opossum gives birth to scarcely developed embryos, which crawl up the mother's fur to a pouch on her underside. There, the baby possum finds one of thirteen teats and settles in to grow for two to three months. It first explores the world by crawling onto its mother's back, where it can be seen riding around with its siblings. The possum defends itself from predators in a variety of ways, but its best-known ploy is to simply keel over and play dead. When humans do this, it's called "playing possum."

OPOSSUM *Didelphis virginiana*

OSPREY

The osprey is a magnificent, fish-eating bird of prey found along the Georgia coast. With a wingspan that can exceed 6 feet, it is easily spotted circling or hovering high above the water. It is well adapted to fishing. Unlike hawks or eagles, which have three fixed forward toes and one opposed, the osprey can move two toes into an opposed position. This versatility comes in handy as it dives below water to catch a slippery fish. It nimbly spins the fish around to a position that offers the least air resistance and flies to a nearby limb for a meal. It can carry fish up to 30 percent of its body weight. Look for its wide nest at the extreme tip of a tree or pole.

OSPREY *Pandion haliaetus*

OYSTER

The oyster is a giving creature. Its meat is a nutritious delicacy. We use its pearl and shiny inner lining for ornament and its shell as a building material. In Georgia, oysters are found in large clumps, called beds, along tidal creeks and estuaries between low and high tidewaters. After hatching, oyster larvae develop a thin translucent shell and have about two weeks to attach themselves to something stable, most often to existing oyster beds. Once they are attached, their shells harden, and they can live up to twenty years. They have many predators, including starfish, shell-drilling snails, and, of course, us. We have enjoyed them since the dawn of history, pausing occasionally to admire the first man who dared toss one down his gullet.

oyster clump

OYSTER *Crassostrea virginica*

PAINTED BUNTING

The male painted bunting is one of the most striking birds in North America. Its plumage is bright blue, red, green, and yellow – like a common finch rolled in the palette of a visionary painter. Painted buntings nest and breed in the spring and summer along Georgia's coast and spend their winters in the Caribbean. Though adults may reach 5½ inches in length, they are hard to spot because they build their nests in dense cover, often in clumps of Spanish moss. The female is dull green but is not without her own distinction – she is the only green member of the finch family.

PAINTED BUNTING *Passerina ciris*

PAWPAW

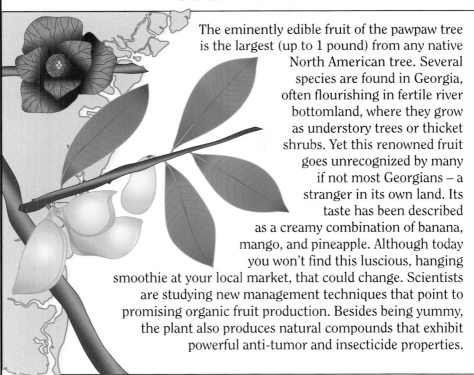

The eminently edible fruit of the pawpaw tree is the largest (up to 1 pound) from any native North American tree. Several species are found in Georgia, often flourishing in fertile river bottomland, where they grow as understory trees or thicket shrubs. Yet this renowned fruit goes unrecognized by many if not most Georgians – a stranger in its own land. Its taste has been described as a creamy combination of banana, mango, and pineapple. Although today you won't find this luscious, hanging smoothie at your local market, that could change. Scientists are studying new management techniques that point to promising organic fruit production. Besides being yummy, the plant also produces natural compounds that exhibit powerful anti-tumor and insecticide properties.

PAWPAW *Asimina triloba*

PIG FROG

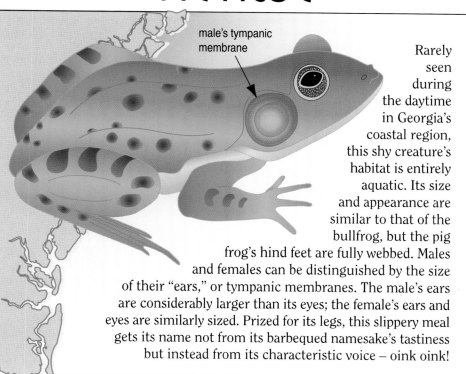

male's tympanic membrane

Rarely seen during the daytime in Georgia's coastal region, this shy creature's habitat is entirely aquatic. Its size and appearance are similar to that of the bullfrog, but the pig frog's hind feet are fully webbed. Males and females can be distinguished by the size of their "ears," or tympanic membranes. The male's ears are considerably larger than its eyes; the female's ears and eyes are similarly sized. Prized for its legs, this slippery meal gets its name not from its barbequed namesake's tastiness but instead from its characteristic voice – oink oink!

PIG FROG *Rana grylio*

PIPEFISH

Several species of this odd creature frequent Georgia's tide marshes. Like its relative the seahorse, the pipefish has an unusual method of reproduction – the male gets pregnant. Through a tube called an ovipositor, the female deposits eggs into a pouch in the male's abdomen. In this brood pouch, the male fertilizes and incubates the eggs.

There, the eggs hatch as embryos and develop into juveniles. As they develop, the pouch becomes large and distended, until Dad looks very pregnant. When the juveniles are developed enough to make their own way in the world, Dad releases them in a cloud of siblings and gets back to being a guy.

CHAIN PIPEFISH *Syngnathus louisianae*

PLANKTON

Plankton are wanderers. Their name comes from a Greek word meaning "that which drifts." The term describes a wide variety of species, both plant and animal, that drift on ocean currents and range in size from single-cell organisms to huge jellyfish. The vast majority are either microscopic or barely visible to the naked eye. Billions of these tiny creatures form the base of the ocean's food chain and produce as much as 80 percent of the free oxygen in the atmosphere. They are crucial to life both in the sea and on land.

PLANKTON

PLANTHOPPER

Planthoppers have two different adult body forms within the same species. Each form has its own males and females. One form is particularly efficient at breeding and reproduction but can't fly. The other form flies but is a less prolific breeder. In summer, both live on the tall, flourishing grass of the low marsh. In the fall, when this tall grass collapses and the population begins to dwindle, the fliers migrate to the short but more stable grass on higher ground. There, most of the fliers' eggs hatch as breeders, who build up the population throughout the winter. But there they are preyed upon relentlessly by spiders, so in spring the fliers migrate back to the low marsh, and the process begins again.

PLANTHOPPER *Prokelisia marginata*

POCKET GOPHER

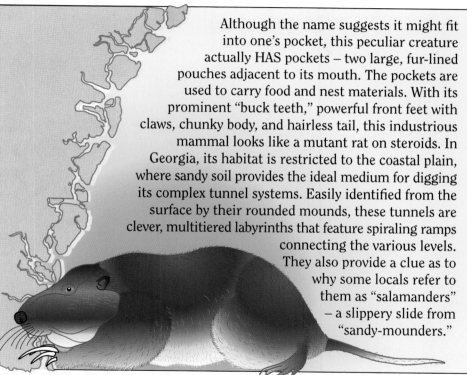

Although the name suggests it might fit into one's pocket, this peculiar creature actually HAS pockets – two large, fur-lined pouches adjacent to its mouth. The pockets are used to carry food and nest materials. With its prominent "buck teeth," powerful front feet with claws, chunky body, and hairless tail, this industrious mammal looks like a mutant rat on steroids. In Georgia, its habitat is restricted to the coastal plain, where sandy soil provides the ideal medium for digging its complex tunnel systems. Easily identified from the surface by their rounded mounds, these tunnels are clever, multitiered labyrinths that feature spiraling ramps connecting the various levels. They also provide a clue as to why some locals refer to them as "salamanders" – a slippery slide from "sandy-mounders."

SOUTHEASTERN POCKET GOPHER *Geomys pinetis*

PORTUGUESE MAN-OF-WAR

The Portuguese man-of-war is armed and dangerous, but its name doesn't tell the whole story. Technically, it should be called "MEN-of-war," since it is not a single creature but a colony of four distinct types of animals, called polyps. Each type of polyp performs a specific function and depends on the others for survival. On top is the float polyp, a bluish bag that secretes and traps gas in order to keep the colony afloat. Below, hang the tentacles, polyps that can reach 45 feet in length. They paralyze prey with a stinging neurotoxin and drag it to the digestive polyps, which, like stomachs, break it down into nutrients. The fourth type of polyp handles reproduction. The man-of-war may be translucent and beautiful above, but danger dangles below. Steer clear of this floating mob scene.

PORTUGUESE MAN-OF-WAR *Physalia physalis*

RESURRECTION FERN

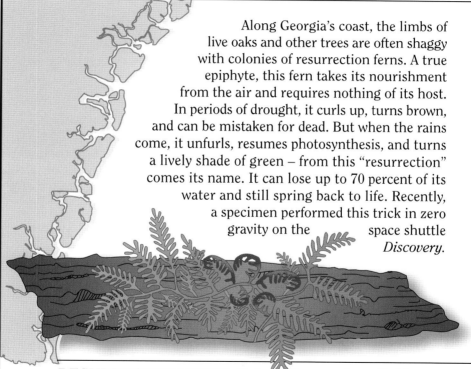

Along Georgia's coast, the limbs of live oaks and other trees are often shaggy with colonies of resurrection ferns. A true epiphyte, this fern takes its nourishment from the air and requires nothing of its host. In periods of drought, it curls up, turns brown, and can be mistaken for dead. But when the rains come, it unfurls, resumes photosynthesis, and turns a lively shade of green – from this "resurrection" comes its name. It can lose up to 70 percent of its water and still spring back to life. Recently, a specimen performed this trick in zero gravity on the space shuttle *Discovery*.

RESURRECTION FERN *Polypodium polypodioides*

RIGHT WHALE

During winter months, the coastal waters off Georgia and northern Florida are the calving grounds for northern right whales. In 1995, this area was designated a critical habitat for this endangered species. Adults reach an average length of 50 feet and weigh about 60 tons. Like other baleen whales, the right whale filters plankton through comb-like teeth. This creature got its name because its body was rich in oil and tended to float after it was killed, making it the "right" whale to hunt. Now this species is so rare that scientists believe it is close to extinction. Clearly, today it is the "right" whale to save.

NORTHERN RIGHT WHALE *Eubalaena glacialis*

RIVER OTTER

This notoriously playful creature's "briar patch" is aquatic. Sleek and graceful, the river otter can be found in a variety of coastal Georgia's aquatic habitats, including the tidal zones of large rivers such as the Altamaha. This clownish carnivore sits atop the food chain and is no joke to its prey — fish, crayfish, frogs, snakes, clams, rodents, and birds. Like other members of the weasel family, it has powerful musk glands that produce an unmistakable "signature" scent — a pungent, if not "scent-sational" means of communicating with other otters.

RIVER OTTER *Lutra canadensis*

SAND DOLLAR

Its name aside, a sand dollar is neither sand nor the currency of mermaids – it is an animal from a class of spiny-skinned marine creatures called echinoids. The bleached white disk that most people refer to as a sand dollar is actually the creature's skeleton. The starlike design on top is made up of five sets of pores, which are used for respiration. Though its skeleton is as smooth as a coin, alive the sand dollar has a velvety skin of tiny spines, which it uses to gather food, burrow in the sand, and move along the ocean floor. Like a real dollar, it has neither legs nor fins but can creep away before you know it.

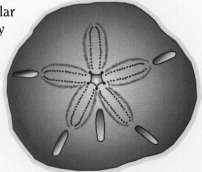

SAND DOLLAR *Mellita quinquiesperforata*

SAND GNAT

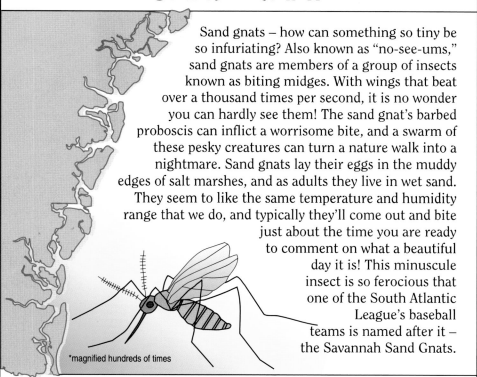

Sand gnats – how can something so tiny be so infuriating? Also known as "no-see-ums," sand gnats are members of a group of insects known as biting midges. With wings that beat over a thousand times per second, it is no wonder you can hardly see them! The sand gnat's barbed proboscis can inflict a worrisome bite, and a swarm of these pesky creatures can turn a nature walk into a nightmare. Sand gnats lay their eggs in the muddy edges of salt marshes, and as adults they live in wet sand. They seem to like the same temperature and humidity range that we do, and typically they'll come out and bite just about the time you are ready to comment on what a beautiful day it is! This minuscule insect is so ferocious that one of the South Atlantic League's baseball teams is named after it – the Savannah Sand Gnats.

*magnified hundreds of times

SAND GNAT *Culicoides furens*

SAND TIGER SHARK

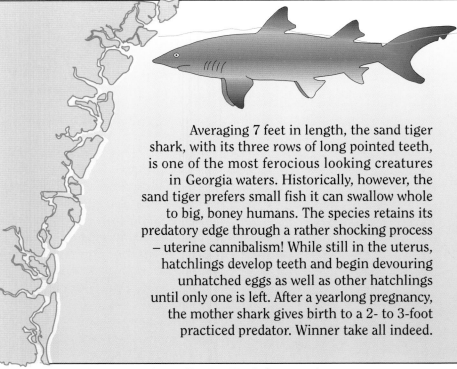

Averaging 7 feet in length, the sand tiger shark, with its three rows of long pointed teeth, is one of the most ferocious looking creatures in Georgia waters. Historically, however, the sand tiger prefers small fish it can swallow whole to big, boney humans. The species retains its predatory edge through a rather shocking process – uterine cannibalism! While still in the uterus, hatchlings develop teeth and begin devouring unhatched eggs as well as other hatchlings until only one is left. After a yearlong pregnancy, the mother shark gives birth to a 2- to 3-foot practiced predator. Winner take all indeed.

SAND TIGER SHARK *Odontaspis taurus*

SARGASSUM

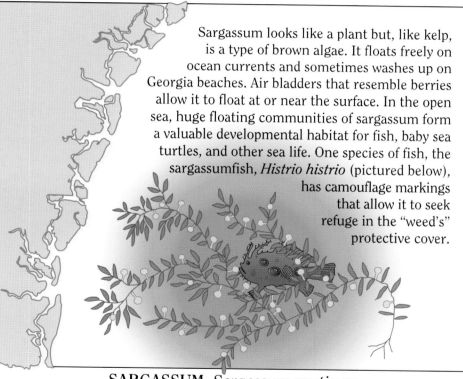

Sargassum looks like a plant but, like kelp, is a type of brown algae. It floats freely on ocean currents and sometimes washes up on Georgia beaches. Air bladders that resemble berries allow it to float at or near the surface. In the open sea, huge floating communities of sargassum form a valuable developmental habitat for fish, baby sea turtles, and other sea life. One species of fish, the sargassumfish, *Histrio histrio* (pictured below), has camouflage markings that allow it to seek refuge in the "weed's" protective cover.

SARGASSUM *Sargassum muticum*

SAW PALMETTO

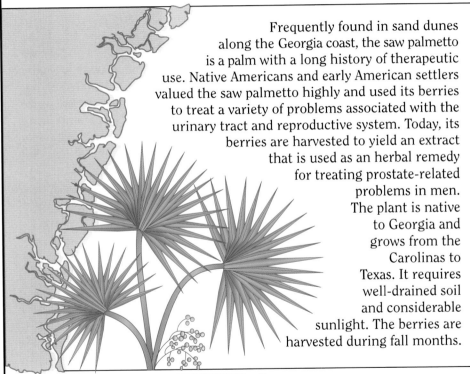

Frequently found in sand dunes along the Georgia coast, the saw palmetto is a palm with a long history of therapeutic use. Native Americans and early American settlers valued the saw palmetto highly and used its berries to treat a variety of problems associated with the urinary tract and reproductive system. Today, its berries are harvested to yield an extract that is used as an herbal remedy for treating prostate-related problems in men. The plant is native to Georgia and grows from the Carolinas to Texas. It requires well-drained soil and considerable sunlight. The berries are harvested during fall months.

SAW PALMETTO *Serenoa repens*

SEA ANEMONE

Feared for their stings, Georgia's anemones are not dangerous to humans. For smaller prey, however, this voracious bigmouth spells trouble! Anemones attach themselves to a firm substrate and then wait for dinner! Their polyp body form is radially symmetrical. They look like a huge mouth on a stem surrounded by tentacles. The tentacles are equipped with microscopic stingers called nematocysts. When unsuspecting prey comes too close, the anemone zaps it with its stingers and then uses its tentacles to stuff its face – all without moving from its place. It's fair to say the anemone never gets its meals "to go."

SEA ANEMONE *Bunodosoma cavernata*

SEA CUCUMBER

Although they are related, sea cucumbers, with their flabby, cylindrical bodies and "warty" skin, bear little resemblance to other echinoderms such as sea stars and sea urchins. Upon closer examination, the "warts" actually are tube feet that serve a number of important functions, from attachment and locomotion, to respiration and gathering food. With a habitat not restricted by ocean depth, sea cucumbers are common to oceans around the world. Three of the more than one thousand known species are found in Georgia waters. Sea "cukes" have a variety of defense mechanisms involving chemical toxins, and their predators often find themselves in quite a "pickle" after realizing, perhaps, that they've bitten off more than they can chew!

BROWN SEA CUCUMBER *Sclerodactyla briareus*

SEAHORSE

With its head at a right angle to its armored body, this fish cuts quite an unusual figure as it propels itself slowly through the water in an upright position. Its horselike upper half tapers into a prehensile tail, which it uses to cling to grasses and corals. Like a chameleon, the seahorse changes colors to blend in with its surroundings, a nifty trick for ambushing unwary prey. Inclined to monogamy, seahorse "couples" perform greeting dances each morning to reaffirm their lifelong bond. Look for these sweethearts courting in Georgia's coastal waters.

LINED SEAHORSE *Hippocampus erectus*

SEA ISLAND COTTON

In the first half of the 1800s, cotton was king in Georgia. And in the narrow micro-climate of the Georgia and South Carolina islands grew the most regal cotton of them all, sea island cotton. This cotton had long, thin fibers that were particularly strong. Almost all of it was exported to Europe, where it was used to make luxurious fabric for the wealthy. This premium cotton brought especially hard work to slaves and often great wealth to planters. From 1790 to 1861 many Georgia and South Carolina islands were given over to its production. It all ended in 1861 when Union forces blockaded Southern ports and then seized that year's exceptional crop. The crop was sold in New York, and the proceeds were used in the war against the planters who grew it.

SEA ISLAND COTTON *Gossypium barbadense*

SEA OATS

The dominant dune builder in coastal Georgia, sea oats are also referred to as "pioneer plants" for their role in creating and stablizing sand dunes. This hardy grass grows in clumps at the edge of the sea. Loose sand is trapped in its stalks and gradually accumulates until the plants are completely covered. Sea oats, however, possess the ability to grow upright even if buried, so eventually new shoots emerge, and the process is repeated until a small hillock is established. As adjacent hillocks merge, dunes are formed. Sea oats create a dense turf that stablizes the dunes. If these plants are removed, the sand blows away. Protect Georgia's pioneer plants – they are not merely dune builders but guardians as well.

SEA OATS *Uniola paniculata*

SEA SQUIRT

Rough sea squirts make their own clothes. They are part of a group of marine animals called tunicates, which secrete for themselves an outer coat, or tunic, of cellulose. At odds with current trends on the fashion runway, this bulb-shaped garment is tough, grisly, warty, and rigid. Note its two simple openings. One admits water bearing food and oxygen. The other expels water and waste. Inside this roomy and functional little number, natural fibers called cilia create a current that directs food particles and tiny organisms to the stomach. When disturbed, the sea squirt is no model for behavior. It contracts and squirts water out of its waste opening. In Georgia, look for it to be bathin' and misbehavin', attached to piers, rocks, and jetties.

ROUGH SEA SQUIRT *Styela plicata*

SHERMAN'S FOX SQUIRREL

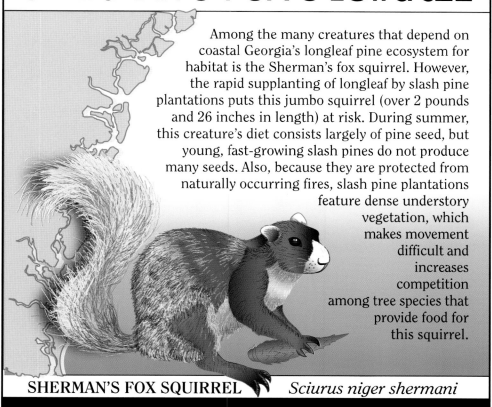

Among the many creatures that depend on coastal Georgia's longleaf pine ecosystem for habitat is the Sherman's fox squirrel. However, the rapid supplanting of longleaf by slash pine plantations puts this jumbo squirrel (over 2 pounds and 26 inches in length) at risk. During summer, this creature's diet consists largely of pine seed, but young, fast-growing slash pines do not produce many seeds. Also, because they are protected from naturally occurring fires, slash pine plantations feature dense understory vegetation, which makes movement difficult and increases competition among tree species that provide food for this squirrel.

SHERMAN'S FOX SQUIRREL *Sciurus niger shermani*

THE SHIFTING SHORE

MOUNTAINS

PIEDMONT

FALL LINE

COASTAL PLAIN

One of the most amazing things about Georgia's coast is that it moves. Fluctuations in global temperature freeze or melt water from the earth's polar ice caps, thus lowering or raising sea level. At the height of a warming trend 40 million years ago, Georgia's beaches were along a band of low hills called the fall line, which runs from Augusta to Macon to Columbus. But during the last Ice Age, the coastline shifted southeast, leaving the sites of Savannah and Brunswick 50 to 60 miles inland. If you wonder which way the shore is headed now, note the extent to which beach-front houses on Saint Simon's Island must armor themselves against the sea.

SHORT-EARED OWL

Also known as a marsh or swamp owl, the short-eared owl winters in the Georgia marshes. A large bird with a wingspan of 42 inches, short-eared owls feed at dawn and dusk on a diet consisting primarily of rodents, although sometimes they will eat bats, birds, and rabbits. As their name suggests, their ear tufts are hardly visible. It is fair to say that unlike other owls, short-ears don't "give a hoot." Instead, they tend to utter harsh nasal barks and squeals.

SHORT-EARED OWL *Asio flammeus*

SHRIMP LIFE CYCLE

Shrimp are Georgia's most economically important fishery, and while most shrimp are caught far offshore, their life cycle reveals the crucial interdependence of rivers, wetlands, and the sea. Adult shrimp breed in deep offshore waters, where each female can release as many as a million eggs. These eggs hatch into larvae that are carried inland by currents. Along the way, they go through several larval stages. A lucky few reach the protection of nursery grounds in tidal creeks and marshes.

There they thrive and grow on a rich soup of marsh nutrients. In two to four months, as juveniles, they begin to crawl along the bottom back out to deep waters to begin the cycle again, unless, of course, they end up in a spicy dollop of cocktail sauce.

SHRIMP LIFE CYCLE

SMOOTH CORDGRASS

If you've seen Georgia's salt marshes, you've seen cordgrass. It is the predominant plant in the magnificent "sea of grass" that grows between Georgia's barrier islands and the mainland. Its importance to the marsh cannot be overstated. Cordgrass filters heavy metals and toxins from the water. It provides habitat for numerous species of fish and shellfish and gives refuge to waterfowl and shorebirds. Its matted roots stabilize the soil and, literally, hold the marsh together. Where tides bathe it in rich nutrients, it can reach a height of 8 feet. Higher in the marsh, it may only grow to a foot or so. Regardless of size, cordgrass is the indispensable thread in the marsh's web of natural wonders.

SMOOTH CORDGRASS *Spartina alterniflora*

SOUTHERN STINGRAY

Some people call the stingray a "flattened-out shark," and in fact stingrays and sharks are closely related, belonging to a subclass of fish called elasmobranchs. Both have cartilage for a skeleton instead of bone. But unlike its menacing cousin, the stingray is a gentle thing of beauty. It seems to fly through the water like a big, gracefully undulating wing. But it spends most of its time on the bottom, crunching crustaceans and mollusks with its powerful jaws and grinding teeth. Though not aggressive, it has a toxic barb on its tail, which can be whipped from side to side and upward as a defense against predators.

SOUTHERN STINGRAY *Dasyatis americana*

SPANISH MOSS

Spanish moss is neither Spanish nor moss. It's a native perennial plant in the bromeliad, or pineapple, family. This mysterious festoonery hangs in independent swags from tree limbs in the coastal plain, imparting a picturesque and romantic aspect to groves of live oak and other trees. Though it produces tiny yellow-green flowers in the spring, in other ways it is quite unlike most plants. An epiphyte, it has no connection to the ground or roots in its host tree. Its ever-branching tendrils, which can grow to 25 feet in length, are covered with scales called trichomes. These scales trap moisture and nutrient-laden dust particles from the air – a rare plant that needs no soil, it harvests the wind.

close-up of flower

SPANISH MOSS *Tillandsia usneoides*

STURGEON

Although uncommon, two varieties of sturgeon, the Atlantic and the shortnose, are found in Georgia waters. These ancient species, whose origins date back 70 million years, are anadromous, meaning they migrate from saltwater habitats to spawn in fresh water. Instead of scales, their bodies are covered with five rows of bony plates called scutes, which give them a menacing, armored appearance. Far from dangerous, adults lack teeth but use their snouts to plow the bottom, sucking up a dinner of worms, crustaceans, and mollusks with their unusual tubelike mouths. The female's eggs are especially prized, but if you find them, they'll most likely be in a jar with a label that reads "caviar"!

SHORTNOSE STURGEON *Acipenser brevirostrum*

ATLANTIC STURGEON *Acipenser oxyrhynchus*

SWALLOW-TAILED KITE

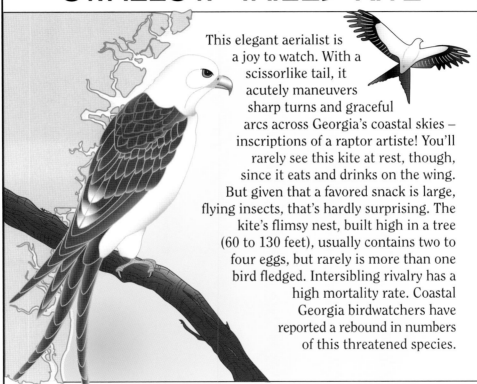

This elegant aerialist is a joy to watch. With a scissorlike tail, it acutely maneuvers sharp turns and graceful arcs across Georgia's coastal skies – inscriptions of a raptor artiste! You'll rarely see this kite at rest, though, since it eats and drinks on the wing. But given that a favored snack is large, flying insects, that's hardly surprising. The kite's flimsy nest, built high in a tree (60 to 130 feet), usually contains two to four eggs, but rarely is more than one bird fledged. Intersibling rivalry has a high mortality rate. Coastal Georgia birdwatchers have reported a rebound in numbers of this threatened species.

AMERICAN SWALLOW-TAILED KITE *Elanoides forficatus*

SWEETGRASS

Sweetgrass is a native perennial that grows in coastal dunes along the Georgia shore. It grows in small clumps and has long, very narrow leaves. Humble and sparse as it is, this grass helped transfer an important African artistic tradition to North America. When Africans were brought to America as slaves, they found the long, strong blades of sweetgrass to be the best local material for continuing their tradition of artful basketry. Used chiefly for ornament today, these baskets were once essential working implements of agriculture. Large deep baskets were used for the harvest and storage of crops, and a flat basket, called a fanner, was used for winnowing rice. These baskets are beautiful heirs to an old and rich tradition.

SWEETGRASS *Muhlenbergia filipes*

TIGER SALAMANDER

Among the largest terrestrial salamanders in the United States, the eastern tiger salamander routinely attains a size of 7 to 8 inches, though this fact is hard to confirm since this creature spends most of its life underground. A member of the group known as "mole salamanders," eastern tigers emerge from their burrows once a year, at night, and find their way to a nearby breeding pond. Once their eggs are fertilized, females deposit clusters and secure them to weed stems underwater. Approximately four weeks later, the eggs hatch into larvae. The larvae transform into sub-adults within several months and leave the pond, again at night and usually during a rain, to make the return journey underground. Stranger still, scientists confirm that the eastern tiger often returns to the same pond in which it was hatched.

EASTERN TIGER SALAMANDER *Ambystoma tigrinum*

WHELK EGG CASING

Beachcombers along Georgia's coast often find a series of disks strung together and protruding from the sand. Most likely this is the egg casing of the knobbed whelk, *Busycon carica*, resident of our official state shell. The coin-shaped disks range in diameter from that of a nickel to that of a quarter and can reach a thickness of ¼ inch. The female whelk can lay a string of these over a foot long. Into each capsule she deposits as many as a hundred eggs along with nutrients. While in the casing, the eggs hatch and the embryos pass through the larval stages and begin to develop a shell. If you hold the casing up to the light you may be able to see the young inside.

KNOBBED WHELK EGG CASING

WILD PIG

This coastal Georgia creature is not a welcome dinner guest. Its eating habits make it a dinner mess instead! Wild pigs, with their efficient shovel-shaped noses, cause extensive damage to all types of ground cover as a result of their manic foraging. These omnivores' quest for food leaves a terrain often resembling an area plowed by a drunk. Keen senses of smell and hearing more than compensate for their notoriously poor eyesight. Largely nocturnal, wild pigs are a formidable foe with their powerful, slashing tusks. Though wild now, they descend from the livestock of European settlers. The wild pigs of Ossabaw Island have remained isolated and are a reasonable facsimile of the domestic pig of 16th-century Spain.

WILD PIG *Sus scrofa*

WOOD STORK

North America's only native stork, the wood stork, is a large, gangly bird with stiltlike legs, a head of exposed black skin, and a long bill that curves downward. It frequents the beaches, marshes, and swamps of Georgia, where it can be seen fishing for food. The wood stork feeds by swinging its open beak back and forth through the water to capture small fish that touch its bill. With a quick snap, "dinner is served."

WOOD STORK *Mycteria americana*

YAUPON HOLLY

The yaupon holly, native to Georgia, is a small evergreen tree that is now cultivated as an ornamental shrub. It makes a beautiful hedge or screen, with white blossoms in spring and red berries in the fall, but a curious cultural practice predates its current suburban usage. The yaupon is the only North American holly that contains caffeine. Indians throughout the Southeast roasted and boiled its leaves to make their famous "Black Tea," which they used as a stimulant at council meetings and before warfare. It was drunk until it acheived a purging effect, as you can gather from its scientific name, *Ilex vomitoria*, even if your Latin is a little rusty. Look for it in the wild along coastal dunes and stream banks.

YAUPON HOLLY *Ilex vomitoria*

ZOEA

At the microscopic level, estuaries teem with fantastical life forms. Though they may look strictly sci-fi, many of these strange creatures, such as blue crab zoea, are just the larval stages of familiar species. After hatching, blue crab zoea float from the estuary out to sea and then back again, changing into seven wildly different shapes along the way. Each shape allows it to feed, move, or protect itself according to its developmental needs. One shape may facilitate voracious feeding, while another allows it to move enough to snag an inward tide. At one stage, it grows a fearsome spike for protection. Four to six weeks after hatching, zoea arrive back at an estuary and finally change into something that resembles the crabs they will become.

BLUE CRAB ZOEA *Callinectes sapidus*

SUGGESTIONS FOR FURTHER READING

Bartram, William. *The Travels of William Bartram.* Edited with commentary and an annotated index by Francis Harper. Athens, Ga.: University of Georgia Press, 1998.

Bertness, Mark D. *The Ecology of Atlantic Shorelines.* Sunderland, Mass.: Sinauer Associates, Inc., 1999.

Bullard, Mary. *Cumberland Island: A History.* Athens, Ga.: University of Georgia Press, 2002.

Georgia Conservancy, The. *A Guide to the Georgia Coast.* Edited by Gwen McKee. Atlanta: Longstreet Press, 1993.

Leigh, Frances Butler. *Ten Years on a Georgia Plantation since the War.* Savannah, Ga.: Library of Georgia, Beehive Press, 1992.

Leigh, Jack. *The Ogeechee.* Athens, Ga.: University of Georgia Press, 1986.

Lenz, Richard J. *Longstreet Highroad Guide to the Georgia Coast and Okefenokee.* Atlanta: Longstreet Press, 1999.

Lombardo, Bruce. *Chew Toy of the Gnat Gods.* Atlanta: Cherokee Publishing Company, 1998.

Price, Eugenia. *St. Simons Memoir.* Philadelphia: Lippincott, 1978.

Ray, Janisse. *Ecology of a Cracker Childhood.* Minneapolis: Milkweed Editions, 1999.

Schoettle, Taylor. *A Guide to a Georgia Barrier Island.* St. Simons Island, Ga.: Watermarks Publishing, 1997.

Seabrook, Charles. *Cumberland Island: Strong Women, Wild Horses.* Winston-Salem, N.C.: J. F. Blair, 2002.

Spornick, Charles D., Alan R. Cattier, and Robert J. Greene. *An Outdoor Guide to Bartram's Travels.* Athens, Ga.: University of Georgia Press, 2003.

Sullivan, Buddy. *Early Days on the Georgia Tidewater: The Story of McIntosh County and Sapelo.* Darien, Ga.: McIntosh County Board of Commissioners, 1997.

Teal, Mildred, and John Teal. *Portrait of an Island.* Athens, Ga.: University of Georgia Press, 1997.

Thomas, David Hurst. *St. Catherines: An Island in Time.* Georgia History and Culture Series. Atlanta: Georgia Humanities Council, 1991.

Vanstory, Burnette. *Georgia's Land of the Golden Isles.* Athens, Ga.: University of Georgia Press, 1981.